POTTY JOK

ISBN-9781090644190

I went to see a fat magician last night

I bet he had a few Twix up his sleeve.

Went to give a sperm sample the other day the nurse said would I like to masturbate in the cup, I said thanks but I don't think I'm ready for a competition yet

What happens when you cross breed a dyslexic agnostic insomniac?

They stay awake all night wondering if there really is a dog.

I need to buy a longer dipstick for my car, mine doesn't reach the oil anymore.

My extra sensitive toothpaste doesn't like it when I use other toothpastes.

I quit my job working for Nike. Just couldn't do it anymore.

A cop just knocked on my door and told me that my dogs were chasing people on bikes. My dogs don't even own bikes.

If you think about it, we chop down bird houses to make bird houses.

I have a chicken proof lawn.

Its impeccable.

I lost my job as a stage designer.

I left without making a scene.

I bought a bag of rocket salad today, it went off before I could eat it

I read that a banana a day helps to keep your colon clean. I just wish they'd told me I was supposed to eat them.

Remember when plastic surgery was a taboo subject? Now you mention Botox and nobody raises an eyebrow.

Not saying we were poor, but many a time my Mother would send me next door with a button, and ask our neighbor if she would sew a shirt on it.

My wife kicked me out because of my terrible Arnold Schwarzenegger impressions.

But don't worry... I'll return!

If women think all men are the same, why do they take so long to choose one?

I learn from the mistakes made by people who took my advice.

There's plenty of fish in the sea, but until I catch one, I'm stuck here just holding my rod.

I spent four hours last night making a belt out of fresh herbs

What a waist of thyme that turned out to be

Don't accept shampoo.

Demand real poo

POTTY JOKES

An old man drove past me on a tractor this morning and told me the end was nigh...

I think it was Farmer Gedden.

Did you know that this week is National Diarrhea Week?

It runs from today until the end Friday

What is the difference between a hippo and a zippo? One is really heavy and the other is a little lighter.

Bad news for agoraphobics,..a cure is just around the corner!

Whats the difference between a good joke and a bad joke timing ?

I just saw a man slumped over a lawn mower crying his eyes out.

He said he'll be fine, he's just going through a rough patch.

How many dyslexics does it take to change a lightbulb?

Steven.

Yesterday, I went to the Air and Space Museum. There was nothing there.

I took a dip in the pool earlier. Stupid really, as I got a load of water in my hummus.

There was a knock at the door this morning, so I opened it and there was a wash basin on the doorstep. I thought, "I'd better let this sink in."

My granddad gave me some sound advice on his deathbed.

"It's always worth investing in a decent set of speakers." he said.

How do you find Will Smith in the snow?

Look for the fresh prints

I was hanging on to the cliff face for dear life.

"Don't look down!" said my friend above me.

So I started smiling.

Got run over by a limo this morning.

It too forever.

DANGER: DO NOT TOUCH must be the scariest thing to read in Braille.

There's nothing that good about Switzerland, really.

Although, their flag is a big plus

POTTY JOKES

I found my first grey pubic hair last night.

That's the last time I'm eating my Grandma's home made Trifle.

I went along to the local Kleptomaniacs Anonymous meeting but all the seats were taken.

Getting old means

A broad mind and a narrow waist change places

During sex you can burn off as many calories as running 5 miles

Who runs 5 miles in 30 seconds ?

Just spent ages waxing the car.

Still not sure how it gets that hairy.

I went on a positive thinking course

It was shit

Here's a tip worth remembering.

If ever you're attacked by a bunch of Clowns, always go for the Juggler.

I was attacked by a Mime Artist yesterday, he did things to me that were unspeakable.

People who can't stop buying full length mirrors need to take a good long look at themselves.

Now that I'm retired, I've taken up meditation. It beats sitting around doing nothing.

I phoned the jaundice clinic.

"Yellow…." said the receptionist.

You know a pessimist is just a well informed optimist?

The film Shrek teaches us that no matter how you look, it's important to find someone who looks as ugly as you.

Remember when jokes weren't just about nostalgia?

Those were the days.

BIG SHOUT OUT to the partially deaf....

They're always telling me to live my dreams. But I don't want to be naked in an exam I haven't revised for.

One of the issues with salad is that it tastes bland.

I think it's a problem that needs addressing.

Never date cross eyed people. They might be seeing somebody on the side!

Got stopped by the cops last night driving home from a bar.

"Any idea why I was following you?", he asked.

"Because my tweets are funny?"

Childproof your house all you want,

they still get in

Working at that Bingo Hall isn't just a job!..It's a calling!

My neighbor has had 44 concussions.

He lives just a stones throw away.

I used to be embarrassed about my geology fetish.

I'm now feeling a little boulder.

I called the Incontinence Hot Line number.

The voice said, "Please hold".

I saw this guy getting jumped by four people so I decided to help.

Now he didn't stand a chance against the five of us?

If you break a mirror with someones head. Who gets the seven years bad luck?

I tried to change my password to '14 days'

The computer said it was two week.

Sentimental.....a perfumed lunatic.

When moths die do they hear a voice telling them to fly towards the light?

My wife is concerned about my addiction to drinking brake fluid but I can stop any time I want.

Have you ever noticed the irony behind 'hyphenated' and 'non-hyphenated' ???

I've just discovered a refreshingly new website "Conjunctivitis.com"

It really is a site for sore eyes

What do you call a Judge with no thumbs?

Justice Fingers!

If at first you don't succeed, sky diving isn't for you!!

My girlfriend just left me because of my pasta fetish.

I'm now feeling cannelloni.

I'm thinking of selling my vacuum.

It's just gathering dust.

Self-important amnesiacs ... who do they think they are?

I'm so self-obsessed I take selfies of myself taking selfies.

My friends reckon that i find any excuse to have a drink.

Speaking of beer........

If you lose one sense your other senses are enhanced.

This is why people with no sense of humor have a heightened sense of self-importance.

POTTY JOKES

I remember the first time I ever saw an Universal Remote Control.

I thought to myself, "Well this changes everything."

How many pessimists does it take to change a lightbulb?

Why bother? The new one will just burn out too.

My girlfriend and I often laugh about how competitive we are. But I laugh more.

There's no "I" in denial.

I don't want to brag, but I do speak a little Latin. I'm not fluent, but I'm sure

if I ever went there, I could get by.

So what if I can't spell Armageddon? It's not the end of the world.

The worst time to have a heart attack is during a game of charades.

My Dad always said "fight fire with fire", which is why he got thrown out of the fire brigade.

The first time I see a jogger smiling, I'll consider it.

Politics is just show business, for ugly people.

My wife just found out I replaced our bed with a trampoline; she hit the roof.

I'm very good friends with 25 letters of the alphabet. I don't know why.

POTTY JOKES

I asked my North Korean friend how it was there, he said he couldn't complain.

When wearing a bikini, women reveal 90 % of their body... men are so polite they only look at the covered parts.

I'm not saying your perfume is too strong. I'm just saying the canary was alive before you got here.

I tried to explain to my 4-year-old son that it's perfectly normal to accidentally poop your pants, but he's still making fun of me.

My girlfriend is always stealing my t-shirts and sweaters... But if I take one of her dresses, suddenly "we need to talk".

Smoking will kill you... Bacon will kill you... But,smoking bacon will cure it.

To this day, the boy that used to bully me at school still takes my lunch money. On the plus side, he makes great Subway sandwiches.

It was only when I bought a motorbike that I found out that adrenaline is brown.

POTTY JOKES

People used to laugh at me when I would say "I want to be a comedian", well nobody's laughing now.

When I told the doctor about my loss of memory, he made me pay in advance.

I named my dog 6 miles so I can tell people that I walk 6 miles every single day.

My grandfather had dementia at 60 and started lathering himself in butter... He went downhill pretty fast after that

The shovel really was a groundbreaking invention.

Then God said unto John: "Come forth and receive eternal life." But John came fifth and won a toaster.

I have an inferiority complex but it's not a very good one.

"I wondered why the baseball was getting bigger. Then it hit me."

POTTY JOKES

One day while in a bank, an old lady asked if I could help her check her balance... so I pushed her over.

You haven't experienced awkward until you try to tickle someone who isn't ticklish.

I have kleptomania, but when it gets bad, I take something for it.

I want to die like my father, peacefully in his sleep, not screaming and terrified, like his passengers.

How come Miss Universe is only ever won by people from Earth?

The problem with kleptomaniacs is that they always take things literally.

It takes a lot of balls to golf the way I do.

I have a friend. He keeps trying to convince me he's a compulsive liar, but I don't believe him.

I'm on a whiskey diet... I've lost three days already.

There's no such thing as addiction, there's only things that you enjoy doing more than life.

I don't worry about terrorism. I was married for two years.

I had a wonderful childhood, which is tough because it's hard to adjust to a miserable adulthood.

A lorry-load of tortoises crashed into a train load of terrapins. What a turtle disaster!

I backed a horse last week at 10 to one. It came in at quarter past four.

I went down to my local supermarket and I said: "I want to make a complaint. This vinegar's got lumps in it". He said: "Those are pickled onions."

I was having dinner with a world chess champion and there was a check tablecloth. It took them two hours to pass the salt.

Four fonts walk into a bar. The barman says: "Oi – get out. We don't want your type in here."

I asked God for a bike, but I know God doesn't work that way. So I stole a bike and asked for forgiveness.

Light travels faster than sound. This is why some people appear bright until you hear them speak.

We never really grow up, we only learn how to act in public.

POTTY JOKES

Knowledge is knowing a tomato is a fruit;
Wisdom is not putting it in a fruit salad.

Politicians and diapers have one thing in common.
They should both be changed regularly, and for
the same reason.

Going to church doesn't make you a Christian any
more than standing in a garage makes you a car.

The early bird might get the worm, but the
second mouse gets the cheese.

My mother never saw the irony in calling me a son-of-a-bitch.

Evening news is where they begin with 'Good evening', and then proceed to tell you why it isn't.

If you think nobody cares if you're alive, try missing a couple of payments.

If God is watching us, the least we can do is be entertaining.

If 4 out of 5 people SUFFER from diarrhea… does that mean that one enjoys it?

Never, under any circumstances, take a sleeping pill and a laxative on the same night.

Did you know that dolphins are so smart that within a few weeks of captivity, they can train people to stand on the very edge of the pool and throw them fish?

I didn't fight my way to the top of the food chain to be a vegetarian

The shinbone is a device for finding furniture in a dark room.

Always borrow money from a pessimist. He won't expect it back.

My psychiatrist told me I was crazy and I said I want a second opinion. He said okay, you're ugly too.

Money can't buy happiness, but it sure makes misery easier to live with.

POTTY JOKES

I got in a fight one time with a really big guy, and he said, "I'm going to mop the floor with your face." I said, "You'll be sorry." He said, "Oh, yeah? Why?" I said, "Well, you won't be able to get into the corners very well."

I always take life with a grain of salt, ...plus a slice of lemon, ...and a shot of tequila.

I cleaned the attic with the wife the other day. Now I can't get the cobwebs out of her hair.

I met a Dutch girl with inflatable shoes last week, phoned her up for a date but she'd popped her clogs.

Went to the doctors and said: "Have you got anything for wind?" He gave me a kite.

A man walks into a bar with a roll of Tarmac under his arm and says: "Pint please, and one for the road."

"Doc, I can't stop singing The Green, Green Grass Of Home." He said: "That sounds like Tom Jones syndrome." "Is it common?" I asked. "It's not unusual," he replied.

Two aerials meet on a roof, fall in love and get married. The reception was brilliant.

POTTY JOKES

Police arrested two kids yesterday. One was drinking battery acid, the other was eating fireworks. They charged one – and let the other one off.

Went to the zoo. There was only one dog in it. It was a shitzu.

A man just assaulted me with milk, cream and butter. How dairy.

Went to the corner shop – bought four corners.

I'll tell you what I love doing more than anything – trying to pack myself in a small suitcase. I can hardly contain myself.

My next-door neighbor worships exhaust pipes, he's a Catholic converter.

Two Eskimos sitting in a kayak were chilly. But when they lit a fire in the craft, it sank, proving once and for all that you can't have your kayak and heat it.

Did you hear about the guy whose whole left side was cut off? He's all right now.

Did you hear about these new reversible jackets?
I'm excited to see how they turn out.

My colleague can no longer attend next week's
Innuendo Seminar so I have to fill her slot instead.

I'm a big fan of whiteboards. I find them quite
re-markable.

I'm reading a horror story in Braille. Something
bad is about to happen... I can feel it.

I bought some shoes from a drug dealer. I don't know what he laced them with, but I've been tripping all day.

Just burned 2,000 calories. That's the last time I leave brownies in the oven while I nap.

Did you hear about the two silk worms in a race? It ended in a tie!

Thanks for explaining the word "many" to me, it means a lot.

The future, the present and the past walked into a bar. Things got a little tense.

I recently heard about a mannequin that lost all of his friends. He was too clothes minded.

My girlfriend told me she was leaving me because I keep pretending to be a Transformer. I said, "No, wait! I can change."

I hate Russian dolls, they're so full of themselves.

I refused to believe my road worker father was stealing from his job, but when I got home all the signs were there.

You can never lose a homing pigeon - if your homing pigeon doesn't come back what you've lost is a pigeon.

As I watched the dog chasing his tail I thought "Dogs are easily amused", then I realized I was watching the dog chasing his tail.

Velcro - what a rip-off!

I've just written a song about tortillas; actually, it's more of a rap.

I had a neck brace fitted years ago and I've never looked back since.

I woke up this morning and forgot which side the sun rises from, then it dawned on me.

I like to hold hands at the movies... which always seems to startle strangers.

I don't have a beer gut. I have a protective covering for my rock hard abs.

I read recipes the same way I read science fiction. I get to the end and I think, 'Well, that's not going to happen.

Money talks. But all mine ever says is goodbye.

I'm skeptical of anyone who tells me they do yoga every day. That's a bit of a stretch.

A clear conscience is usually the sign of a bad memory.

My therapist says I have a preoccupation with vengeance. We'll see about that.

Money can't buy you happiness? Well, check this out, I bought myself a Happy Meal!

I don't have an attitude problem. You have a perception problem.

The problem isn't that obesity runs in your family. The problem is no one runs in your family.

Letting go of a loved one can be hard. But sometimes, it's the only way to survive a rock climbing catastrophe.

A positive attitude may not solve all your problems. But it will annoy enough people to make it worth the effort.

Build a man a fire, and he'll be warm for a day. Set a man on fire, and he'll be warm for the rest of his life.

I used to be indecisive. Now I'm not sure.

Women should not have children after 35. Really, 35 children are enough.

Change is inevitable—except from a vending machine.

It's never a good idea to keep both feet firmly on the ground. You'll have trouble putting on your pants.

Why does someone believe you when you say there are four billion stars but check when you say the paint is wet?

The easiest job in the world has to be coroner. What's the worst thing that could happen? If everything goes wrong, maybe you'd get a pulse.

I have all the money I'll ever need—if I die by 3:00 p.m. this afternoon.

You are such a good friend that, if we were on a sinking ship together and there was only one life jacket, I'd miss you so much and talk about you fondly to everybody who asked.

A bargain is something you don't need at a price you can't resist.

A bus is a vehicle that runs twice as fast when you are after it as when you are in it.

If winning isn't everything why do they keep score?

Good health is merely the slowest possible rate at which one can die.

POTTY JOKES

It is hard to understand how a cemetery raised its burial cost and blamed it on the cost of living.

Why do they lock gas station bathrooms? Are they afraid someone will clean them?

Keep the dream alive: Hit the snooze button.

If you can stay calm while all around you is chaos, then you probably haven't completely understood the situation.

Archaeologist: someone whose career lies in ruins.

Materialism: buying things we don't need with money we don't have to impress people that don't matter.

Progress is made by lazy men looking for an easier way to do things.

See, the problem is that God gives men a brain and a penis, and only enough blood to run one at a time.

A friend is someone who will help you move. A GOOD friend is someone who will help you move a dead body.

Why do we press harder on a remote control when we know the batteries are getting weak?

Why is it called Alcoholics ANONYMOUS when the first thing you do is stand up and say, 'My name is Peter and I am an alcoholic'

Stress is when you wake up screaming and you realize you haven't fallen asleep yet.

What is the most important thing to learn in chemistry?

Never lick the spoon.

No one is listening until you fart.

Drink coffee! Do stupid things faster with more energy!

I was such an ugly kid. When I played in the sandbox the cat kept covering me up.

If I'd shot you sooner, I'd be out of jail by now.

Everything is edible, some things are only edible once.

What has four legs and an arm? A happy pit bull.

One tequila, two tequila, three tequila, floor.

I'm in shape. Round is a shape isn't it

POTTY JOKES

Bills travel through the mail at twice the speed

Never test the depth of the water with both feet.

I have to exercise early in the morning before my brain figures out what I'm doing.

You are depriving some poor village of its idiot.

POTTY JOKES

At every party there are two kinds of people: those who want to go home and those who don't. The trouble is, they are usually married to each other.

Constipated people don't give a crap.

I was thinking about how people seem to read the Bible a whole lot more as they get older. Then it dawned on me… they were cramming for their finals.

Your gene pool could use a little chlorine.

POTTY JOKES

The trouble with doing something right the first time is that nobody appreciates how difficult it was.

Do not walk behind me, for I may not lead. Do not walk ahead of me, for I may not follow. Do not walk beside me either. Just pretty much leave me the hell alone.

Strangers have the best candy.

If I had to describe myself in three words, I would say "Not very good at maths".

How do you get holy water? Boil the hell out of it.

I'd kill for a Nobel Peace Prize.

Why do you need a driver's license to buy liquor when you can't drink and drive?

I bet you I could stop gambling.

How many bad spellcheckers does it take to stew in a slight blob?

If I can give you one piece of advice from my life it would be, never ever date a tennis player!

I don't know why but it's like love means nothing to them!

Who invented the brush they put next to the toilet? That thing hurts!

With a calendar, your days are numbered.

If it's true that we are here to help others, then what exactly are the others here for?

Laugh and the world laughs with you. Snore and you sleep alone

What's the difference between ignorance and apathy?

I don't know and I don't care.

Did you hear about the semi-colon that broke the law? He was given two consecutive sentences.

POTTY JOKES

"'My drug test came back negative. My dealer sure has some explaining to do."

"It became so cold in New York last night that it forced the flashers to describe themselves to people."

"I think it's wrong that only one company makes the game Monopoly."

I think my neighbor is stalking me as she's been googling my name on her computer. I saw it through my telescope last night.

I hate people who use big words just to make themselves look perspicacious.

My email password has been hacked. That's the third time I've had to rename the cat.

You have two parts of brain, 'left' and 'right'. In the left side, there's nothing right. In the right side, there's nothing left.

I was going to look for my missing watch, but I could never find the time.

POTTY JOKES

A dad is washing the car with his son. After a moment, the son asks his father, "Do you think we could use a sponge instead?"

When I found out that my toaster wasn't waterproof, I was shocked.

A girl phoned me the other day and said, "Come on over, there's nobody home." I went over. Nobody was home.

I don't understand why people get attacked by sharks. Can they not hear the music?

POTTY JOKES

Whenever i have a headache,i take two aspirins and keep away the children,like the bottle says

I'm not saying I hate you, but I would unplug your life support to charge my phone.

I used to be in a band, we were called 'lost dog'. You probably saw our posters.

My wife was furious at me for kicking dropped ice cubes under the refrigerator. But now it's just water under the fridge.

The police say that they burn all the weed they confiscate, so that would explain the doughnuts.

I like to play chess with old men in the park although it's hard to find 32 of them

I can never remember what chloroform smells like.

When it comes to double negatives, don't trust no one.

You know you're getting old when on a Friday night you're listening to the police scanner instead of being on it.

I wonder if the guy who coined the phrase 'One Hit Wonder' coined any other phrases.

To whoever stole my antidepressants, I hope you're happy.

You know you're getting old when you're watching a porn movie and think, "Damn, that bed looks comfortable."

A warning to the person who stole my glasses, I have contacts.

That cow has 12 nipples, dozen tit?

I hate sitting in traffic, because I always get run over.

I had a recurring dream once...

My friend is making a lot of money by selling photos of salmon dressed up in human clothes, like shooting fish in apparel.

The saying, "say no to drugs" has always made me laugh, because if you're talking to drugs, it's probably too late to say no to them.

My wife told me to embrace my mistakes so I hugged her.

I used to work in search and rescue, which I always had a flare for

POTTY JOKES

My doc advised me to wash my pupils, but it's not like eye care.

this sedentary lifestyle is just not working out

I ate four cans of alphabet soup and just had the biggest vowel movement ever.

I thought I was drowning in Coca-Cola, but it was only a Fanta sea!

Why is a bra singular and panties plural?

I've woken up over 10,000 times and I'm still not used to it.

BREAKING: A man who took an airline to court after losing his luggage has lost his case.

I tried to lookup "impotence" on the internet, but nothing came up.

I'm inclined to be laid back

I started seeing a psycho-therapist, but he kept killing people, so now I see a regular therapist.

I need to buy a longer dipstick for my car, mine doesn't reach the oil anymore.

If smoking marijuana causes short-term memory loss, what does smoking marijuana do?

I thought about doing some yoga, but then thought, "That's a bit of a stretch."

I met an Irish guy impervious to bullets. His name was Rick O'Shea.

I bought car insurance on my wedding anniversary so I'd get a reminder letter every year.

Birthdays are nice and all, but too many of them can kill you.

Printed in Great Britain
by Amazon

32907137R00043